AF599203

Written by Dennis Shaely
Illustrated by Stephen Schreiber

Visit us at
SequoiaKidsMedia.com
for bonus
downloadable content

Photography © Shutterstock 2022 Lasse Ansaharju; Jeffrey B. Banke; Petr Bonek; Shllabadibum Bubidibam; cctm; Wynn Dhyana; Georgia Evans; Fotokostic; Four Oaks; Groomee; mark higgins; Eric Isselee; Juliarchit; Katiekk; kontrymphoto; Kwadrat; Lenkadan; Magnifical Productions; mariait; NiP STUDIO; PeopleImages.com - Yuri A; August Phunitiphat; Pukhov K; Anastasija Popova; Vanessa van Rensburg; Sascha Richardson; Vova Shevchuk; smereka; SritanaN; Stockimo; Taylored Photos; TristanBM

Published by Sequoia Kids Media,
an imprint of Sequoia Publishing & Media, LLC

Sequoia Publishing & Media, LLC,
a division of Phoenix International Publications, Inc.

8501 West Higgins Road, Chicago, Illinois 60631
34 Seymour Street, London W1H 7JE
Heimhuder Straße 81, 20148 Hamburg

Customer Service: CS@SequoiaKidsBooks.com

www.SequoiaKidsMedia.com

Library of Congress Control Number: 2022920261

ISBN: 979-8-7654-0179-8

TABLE OF CONTENTS

WHO are horses?

Horses belong to the species Equus caballus. They are hardy, four-legged mammals. Each leg has one toe that is protected by a hard covering, called a hoof, which is similar to a really thick toenail.

IT'S A FACT!

First domesticated, or tamed, by people almost 6,000 years ago, these strong animals have been bred to help us everywhere from the farm to the battlefield. Since then, horses have also been raised for sport and show.

DID YOU KNOW?

Horses, zebras, and donkeys are all related. They belong to the same animal family that scientists call Equidae. A mule is a crossbreed of a horse and a donkey.

HOW many types of horses are there?

While there are many different kinds, or breeds, of horses, they can be divided into three main groups: heavy horses, light horses, and ponies.

Heavy horse

WHO are heavy horses?

Large, muscular horses are called heavy breeds. They are usually the biggest and tallest horses. Originally bred in northern Europe during the Middle Ages, they were used for carrying heavy loads and pulling plows to till fields. The heavy horses were also used for battle. Sometimes they wore armor just like the medieval knights who rode them! They are still used today for plowing, logging, and showing.

WHO are light horses?

Light horses are smaller and thinner looking than the heavy breeds. They are bred for speed, agility, and stamina. Some light horses are used for work such as pulling carriages and ranching, while others are used for racing and show competitions.

WHO are ponies?

Ponies are often thought to be baby horses, but they are actually breeds of horses that are much shorter—even when fully grown.

WHAT do horses look like?

Horses' eyes sit high on their long heads. They are positioned to give horses a wide field of vision, which is perfect for seeing other animals sneaking up from the sides or behind to hunt them for food. But their eyes also face forward so horses can see whatever might be in front of them.

IT'S A FACT!

Horses' ears, also high on their heads, can be controlled independently to allow them to figure out where sounds are coming from.

HOW do horses use their sense of smell?

Like many other animals, horses use their sense of smell to help them find food and water—and to recognize family, friends, and enemies.

DID YOU KNOW?

Horses use their tails to swat away pesky insects.

HOW big are horses?

Horses are measured in hands from the ground to their withers—the ridge between their shoulders. A hand is about 4 inches (10.2 centimeters) long, which is about the width of an adult's hand.

American saddlebred (average height: 15 to 16 hands)

Shetland pony (average height: 9.3 hands)

IT'S A FACT!

Ponies are generally less than 14.2 hands (14 hands plus 2 inches) high and most light horses are 14.2 to 16 hands high. Heavy breeds usually stand more than 16 hands high.

DID YOU KNOW?

Averaging 17 hands high, the Shire is the largest horse. The tallest horse ever recorded was a Shire named Sampson, later renamed Mammoth, who stood more than 21.25 hands high—that's more than 7 feet!

Shire (average height: 17 hands)

HORSE MEASUREMENT CHART:

- 1 hand = 4 inches (10.2 cm)
- 14.2 hands = 58 inches (147.3 cm)
- 16 hands = 64 inches (162.6 cm)

HOW do horses live?

Horses are social animals. In the wild, they live with their families in large groups called herds. Most herds are made up of male and female horses, but some are all male. A dominant male horse who can breed, called a stallion, usually leads the herd. The stallion acts as the protector.

Przewalski's horse

DID YOU KNOW?

There are very few types of undomesticated horses left in the world. Only the Przewalski's horse of Mongolia and untamed horses, called feral horses, still roam free.

IT'S A FACT!

Feral horses are often called wild horses, but they come from domestic horse breeds and are not truly wild animals.

WHAT do horses eat?

Horses are herbivores, which means they do not eat meat. They mostly graze on grass. Although grass is not very nutritious for people, it has everything horses need to stay strong and healthy.

HORSE FOOD:
• Grass
• Hay and grains (on farms)
• Other plants
IT'S A FACT!
Horses' mouths and front teeth are especially well formed for eating grass right from the ground. Their long jaws are lined with teeth that grind the grass to a fine pulp, making it easy to swallow and digest.

HOW do horses grow?

Fast! Female horses, called mares, usually give birth to one baby at a time. Newborn horses, called foals, can usually stand up within an hour of being born. Their legs may be unsteady at first, but soon they will be able to keep up with their mother at nearly full speed.

Pony mare

IT'S A FACT!

Horses less than four years old are called colts. Sometimes female horses in this age range are called fillies.

WHAT do foals eat?

Like all mammals, foals drink milk from their mothers. To get extra nutrition, they may nurse for up to a year, although they start eating grass within a few weeks of being born.

Finnhorse mare

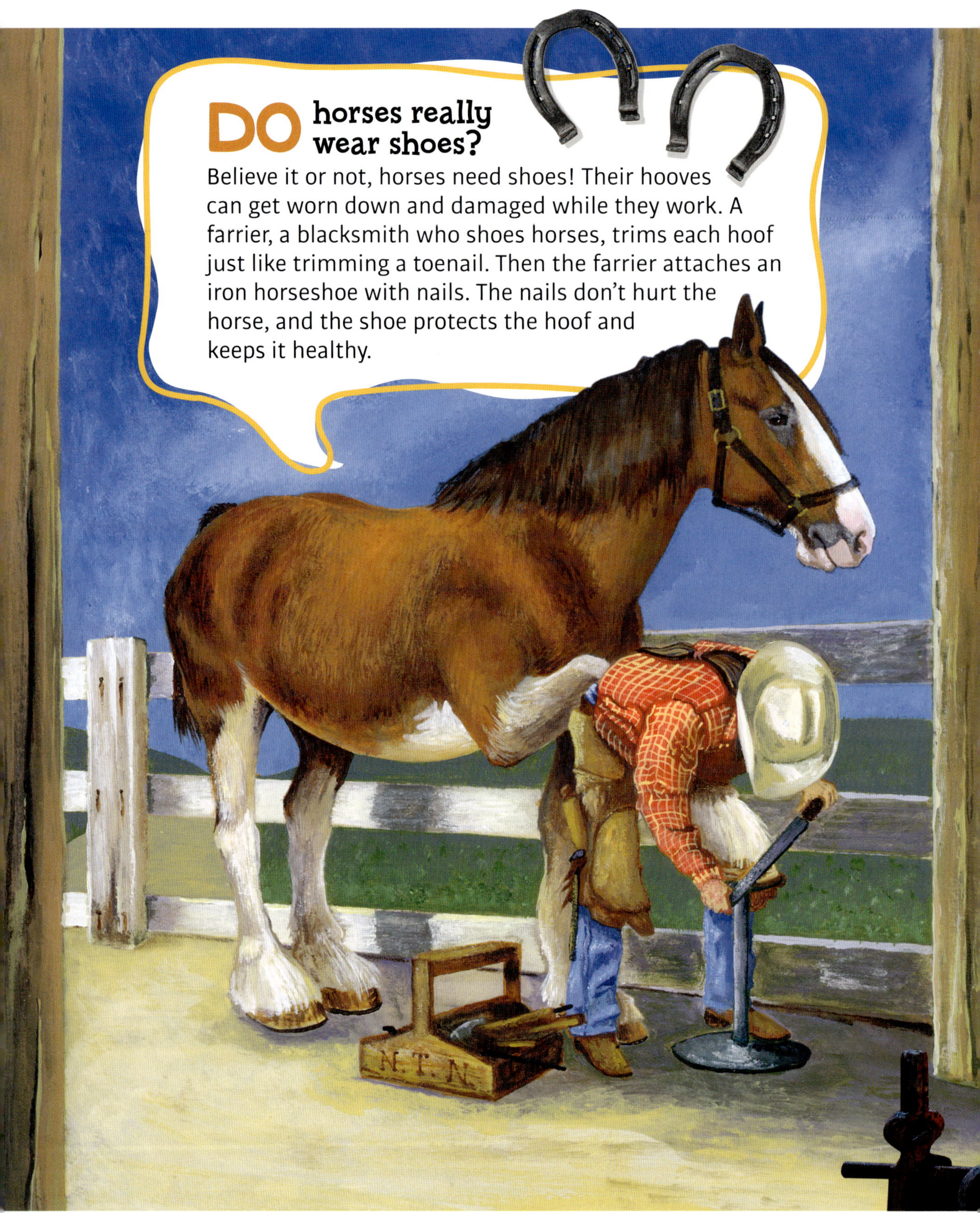

DO horses really wear shoes?

Believe it or not, horses need shoes! Their hooves can get worn down and damaged while they work. A farrier, a blacksmith who shoes horses, trims each hoof just like trimming a toenail. Then the farrier attaches an iron horseshoe with nails. The nails don't hurt the horse, and the shoe protects the hoof and keeps it healthy.

DID YOU KNOW?
Horseshoes have been considered a sign of good luck for hundreds of years. According to one legend, Saint Dunstan the blacksmith gave the horseshoe special power against evil.
IT'S A FACT!
A blacksmith is someone who makes things out of metal by hand. Many farriers have some blacksmithing knowledge to make horseshoes!

HOW do horses communicate?

Horses spend much of their time grooming each other to show affection, form friendships, and help each other clean up. But a horse may also nip at another horse to try to show that it is in charge.

Two domestic palominos fighting each other to decide who's boss

DID YOU KNOW?

All horses can sleep standing up. This allows them to quickly run away from predators because they don't have to get up off the ground and to their feet. But horses also rest and sleep lying down when they feel safe and comfortable.

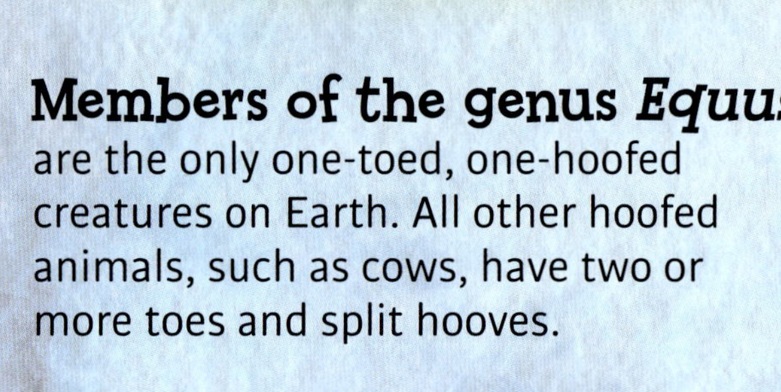

Members of the genus *Equus* are the only one-toed, one-hoofed creatures on Earth. All other hoofed animals, such as cows, have two or more toes and split hooves.

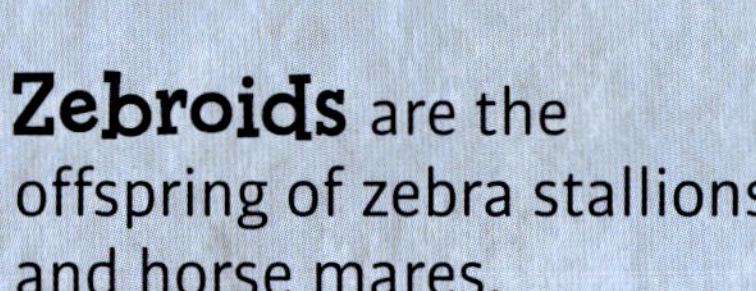

Zebroids are the offspring of zebra stallions and horse mares.

Pegasus is a famous horse from Greek mythology. Unlike real horses, Pegasus had wings and could fly!

Horses were once such an important part of life that the first trains were called iron horses and the first automobiles were called horseless carriages. Even today, the word "horsepower" is used to describe how much work a machine can do!

HORSES ARE AMAZING!

They have been our helpers and companions for thousands of years. Though engine-powered machines have replaced these animals in many ways, don't say happy trails to horses anytime soon—grass will always be cheaper than gas!